Influential Political Systems and Philosophers in History

By Tibor Machan

Chapman University

Bassim Hamadeh, Publisher
Michael Simpson, Vice President of Acquisitions
Christopher Foster, Vice President of Marketing
Jessica Knott, Managing Editor
Stephen Milano, Creative Director
Kevin Fahey, Cognella Marketing Program Manager
Marissa Waggoner, Acquisitions Editor
Kevin Hoffman, Project Editor

Copyright © 2012 by University Readers, Inc. All rights reserved. No part of this publication may be reprinted, reproduced, transmitted, or utilized in any form or by any electronic, mechanical, or other means, now known or hereafter invented, including photocopying, microfilming, and recording, or in any information retrieval system without the written permission of University Readers, Inc.

First published in the United States of America in 2012 by University Readers, Inc.

Trademark Notice: Product or corporate names may be trademarks or registered trademarks, and are used only for identification and explanation without intent to infringe.

15 14 13 12 11   1 2 3 4 5

Printed in the United States of America

ISBN: 978-1-60927-281-4

www.cognella.com 800.200.3908

Contents

Introduction	1
Current Live Political Options	3
Summary of Political Philosophers	15
Conclusion	27

Introduction

Since before Socrates' era in ancient Athens, people have wondered how to organize human communities.

The topic was eventually called "politics," after the term used by Aristotle to designate an organized human community in his treatise, *Politics*: namely, the *polis*.

The question that political philosophy addresses, at least as we now understand it,[1] concerns how to live in each others' company simply by virtue of its being a human community, not some special community (such as an academic society, a rowing club, or a labor union).

This discussion will focus on some—by no means even a fully representative sample—of the influential political systems proposed on the subject of political philosophy throughout human history, most of them live options around the globe today.

---

1 In the writings of Leo Strauss, in contrast, "political philosophy" is used to mean being prudent about philosophy, or managing philosophy in a politic or shrewd way. See Leo Strauss, *What is Political Philosophy? and Other Studies* (Glencoe, IL: Free Press, 1959).

Current Live Political Options

Conservatism

This is a certain way of doing politics and public policy: that is, by paying the closest attention to the prevailing ideas of the past. These are deemed to be tried and true, and should never be abandoned unless absolutely necessary. To "conserve" is the best policy.

Radicalism

This is doing politics and public policy by going to the root of things, to the most basic ideas, and deriving principles from there. Never mind about the past, what counts is what is logically derived from the most fundamental things.

Liberalism

This is not a method but a substantive doctrine that favors some version of human liberty (negative or positive—more on that later).

Monarchism

In this system, there is a supreme authority above society whose dictates must be followed, because they come from an inspired ruler (who is often advised by God).

Theocratic Feudalism

Although not so familiar in the West, the feudal system of social and political life was once extremely popular. Some places across the globe are still organized in line with it, mostly in compliance with edicts found in various religious texts such as the *Koran*.

In a feudal order, vassals hold land and serfs do the work on it, in return for which they provide overlords with military and other services and pay (taxes). The feudal system involves a hierarchical social structure, usually with a monarch or other supreme ruler or family in charge, and various layers of nobility in gradually descending order of importance, with the serfs comprising the bottom. It was the predominant type of order of Europe, and indeed, much of the world, and many of the legal features of contemporary societies can be traced to it.[1] This system of government derives largely from historical events and certain prominent ideas advanced in various philosophical and theological systems, including the notion that some people are naturally, or by divine edict, superior in moral and other respects to the rest, and ought, therefore, to have a paternalistic relationship to them. A form of elitism—the entrenched superiority and often rule of the select few—is usually at the bottom of the feudal ideal, including aristocracy (although since this means the rule of the best, there is some ambiguity about whether it can support anything that is entrenched or static, since who the best are could change drastically over time).

In a feudal system, also, major social institutions—commerce, religion, property holdings, and professional positions—are usually assigned from above, by the designees of the royal family. Accordingly, the economic system of mercantilism is closely linked to feudalism, as is the institution of a state church. (Although, often the prevailing church authorities can be separated from the state. This can give rise to complex dilemmas of spiritual and political leadership.)

It is fair to say that the idea of a constitution arose, in part, in opposition to feudal rule, so we will consider it next. It is also arguable that a modern version of feudalism is fascism, in which an inspired leader rises to political leadership and gains the citizenry's trust to do the right thing for the country, not by following some plan, but by relying on personal insight and wisdom.

---

[1] For example, the police power of states derives from the idea that the head of the feudal order is the "keeper of the realm," and must make sure that the lives of people within a given jurisdiction are well taken care of materially, spiritually, and morally.

Constitutionalism

The term "constitution" derives from the verb "to constitute." This means "to be the basic structure" of something. Thus, a constitutional system of government usually involves having a written document as the basis for governmental decisions. When one hears the slogan "government by law, not by men," this pertains to the idea that a constitution must guide what those in charge of government will do, and that men can be held accountable for how they govern—they are not absolute rulers who do what they personally want or deem right.

Constitutionalism could be connected with a monarchy or with a democracy. Although in our time, in the bulk of the world it is constitutional democracy that is usually instituted as the system of government. There has been much experimentation with constitutional monarchy. (A parliamentary system is also a form of partly decentralized rule by council via the participation of political representatives from various regions of a country.) Usually, constitutions will list basic principles of decision making and of the limits of power or authority of the governing administration. In the United States, for example, the federal Constitution has within it a Bill of Rights that provides a list of limits on the government's authority and scope.

Such a system is usually recommended, because of the predictability of the rules that govern the lives of people within a given geographical area. Yet, since there is no way to predict for the long range what problems will face people, the Constitution usually needs to be interpreted to apply to topics that were not in evidence when it was originally drafted. A great deal of controversy surrounds just how this process should be implemented. The United States has the system of judicial review. If the legislature or other lawmaking bodies proposed policies that some see as conflicting with the Constitution, the matter can be brought to the attention, ultimately, of the U.S. Supreme Court. A judgment could then be forthcoming as to whether this measure accords with or violates the Constitution—in other words, whether it is legal.

Another source of controversy about constitutionalism is whether it is ultimately democratic, whether it does justice to the idea that government must be *by the people*. A constitution stretches the ideas and ideals of the drafters or framers way into the future, past their own lives and citizenship. As such, some have claimed that constitutions are dictatorial and undemocratic. It is also claimed, in criticism of constitutionalism, that it makes permanent (or at least unreasonably influential) the moral and political misconceptions or narrow-mindedness of the past. Unless some handy way of making moral and political adjustments is part of the constitution itself, this can become a debilitating aspect of constitutional government and issue in civil upheaval.

Yet without some basic document by which citizens are governed, government would arguably degenerate into arbitrary rule, by the judgments and the passions of either a monarch or the people. This is why it is usually championed by its supporters, such as the American founders (as per their long discussion of the matter in *Cato's Letters* and The Federalist Papers).

Socialism

In modern political theory, the influence of economic considerations has loomed very large. Among the views that dwell a good deal on the economic features of human communities, socialism is foremost. As such, it is most often defined as the political economic order within which the means of production are publicly owned and usually administered by government.

Yet, socialism is actually a system focused on the nature of human life as a whole. Socialists see the human being as part of a large whole, society or even humanity. As Marx claimed, "The human essence is the true collectivity of man,"[2] meaning that a human being is a specie-being, the kind that is fully aware of belonging to "the organic body"[3] of humanity.

Although not all Socialists stress the collective nature of human life, most would agree that human beings are basically part of society, and cannot be understood—let alone flourish—apart from others. Not only that, but their mutual flourishing is a precondition of the flourishing of each individually. Thus, the privatization of human life is at best a historical stage, and at worst a complete distortion of what human living requires. Private property, for example, or individual rights more generally, conflicts with the proper mode of human living; thus, in any system that involves the legal affirmation of privacy, human beings will be alienated.[4]

The stress in socialism is laid on the health of society or humanity as a whole, although this cannot be separated from the well-being of the constituent parts: namely the individual human beings who comprise the larger wholes. What in particular needs to characterize a good or just human community is cooperation, as opposed to competition or rivalry, in all realms of life—economic, scientific, political, and athletic. In that most important realm, the economic, socialism proposes the collectivization of the administration of all production and distribution of value (although such administration does not preclude subjecting some spheres of economic life to limited competition, a policy that is dubbed "market socialism"). So while Socialists do not necessarily embrace the idea of central microeconomic management and planning, they do favor the supervision of society's economic affairs from the viewpoint of the public at large, with private initiative taking a subservient role. The idea is that only when human beings collectively manage their economic lives will they experience themselves as fully emancipated, coming into their own full humanity or realizing their true human nature. The reason is that, by nature, human beings are conscious producers. Since

---

[2] Karl Marx, *Selected Writings*, ed., David McLellan (London, England: Oxford University Press, 1977), p. 126.

[3] Karl Marx, *Grundrisse*, trans. ed., David McLellan (New York: HarperTorchbooks, 1971), p. 33.

[4] For extended discussions of these issues, see Tibor R. Machan, ed., *The Main Debate, Communism versus Capitalism* (New York: Random House, 1988).

production is necessarily a social phenomenon, only if people participate in the social organization of production can they experience themselves as they truly are.

Socialism can take several forms. Some claim that, at least at the beginning of a Socialist society, there must be central planning by those who understand the need for socialism, helping thereby to upgrade those who are lagging behind in their awareness of this need. Some would want a more democratic socialism, whereby members of the community set priorities for the whole, in a kind of ongoing conversation about the priorities. Some others, as already suggested, see only a limited need for socialization of economic and other matters, albeit one that is vital (mostly as far as the satisfaction of basic human needs are concerned).

Just like human language, so human life in general must be seen as a social process. The idea that we can make a significant difference to our lives as individuals is just as much of a mistake as the idea that we can invent our own language. That is perhaps one of the key reasons for claiming that socialism is the proper form of human social life.

Libertarianism and Capitalism

Libertarianism is the political system wherein the highest political good is the protection of the individual citizen's right to life, liberty, and property. Capitalism is the economic system of libertarianism, since in libertarian societies, the institution of the right to private property, that is, to own anything of value (not, of course, other human beings, who are themselves owners), is fully respected and protected.

Libertarian law rests on the idea that the individual is the most important member of society, with all groups to be formed by the consent of individual members, including the military, corporations, universities, clubs, and the government itself. What is primarily prohibited in a libertarian society is involuntary servitude. What is primarily promoted via the political administration is the liberty of all persons to advance their own objectives, provided they do not violate anyone's equal rights in the process.

There is dispute about the label "capitalism" as the proper way to call the economic order under libertarianism, mostly because its definition is often a precondition of having either a favorable or unfavorable view of the system. Some have insisted on the use of "laissez-faire," in memory of the French entrepreneurs who responded to the king's question as to what the government can do to help the economy, by exclaiming: "Laissez-faire, laissez passer," or "Allow us to do, allow us to act." Some use F. A. Hayek's term "the spontaneous order" to stress such a system's support of uncoerced behavior. There is also the more popular term "free enterprise." Yet capitalism is most widely used, by both critics and supporters of an economic order in which individuals have the right to own property and the use of it on their own terms.

By itself, capitalism is an *economic* arrangement of an organized human community, or polity. Often, however, entire societies are called capitalist, mainly to stress their thriving commerce and industry. More rigorously understood, however, capitalism presupposes a libertarian legal order governed by the rule of law, in which the principle of private property rights plays a central role. Such a system of laws was historically grounded on various *classical liberal* ideals in political thinking. These ideals can be defended by means of positivism, utilitarianism, and natural rights theory and/or individualism, as well as notions about the merits of laissez-faire (no government interference in commerce), the "invisible hand" (as a principle of spontaneous social organization), prudence and industriousness (as significant virtues), the price system, as distinct from central planning (for registering supply and demand), etc.

Put a bit differently, "capitalism," or "libertarianism," is the term used to mean that feature of a human community whereby citizens are understood to have the basic right to make their own (more or less wise or prudent) decisions concerning what they will do with their labor and property, whether they will engage in trade with one another involving nearly anything they may value. Thus, capitalism includes freedom of trade and contract, the free movement of labor, and the protection of property rights against both criminal and official intrusiveness.

The concept "freedom" plays a central role in the understanding of both libertarianism and capitalism. There are two prominent ways of understanding the nature of freedom as it pertains to human relationships. The one that fits with capitalism is *negative* freedom: the condition of everyone in society not being ruled by others with respect to the use and disposal of themselves and what belongs to them. Citizens are free, in this sense, when no other adult person has authority over them that they have not granted of their own volition. In short, in capitalism, one enjoys negative freedom, which amounts to being free *from* others' intrusiveness. The other meaning of freedom is that citizens have their goals and purposes supported by others or the government in order to prosper. Under this conception of freedom, one is free to progress, advance, develop, or flourish only when one is enabled to do so by the efforts of capable others.

In international political discussions, the concept "capitalist" is used very loosely, to the extent that such very diverse types of societies as Italy, New Zealand, the United States of America, Sweden, and France are all considered capitalist. Clearly, no country today is completely capitalist. None enjoys a condition of economic *laissez-faire* in which governments stay out of people's commercial transactions except when conflicting claims over various valued items are advanced, and the dispute needs to be resolved in line with due process of law. But many Western-type societies protect a good deal of free trade, even if they also regulate most of it as well. Still, just as those countries are called "democratic" if there is substantial suffrage—even though many citizens may be prevented from voting—so if there exists substantial free trade and private ownership of the major means of production (labor, capital, intellectual creations, etc.), the country is usually designated as capitalist.

The most common reason among political economists for supporting capitalism is this system's support of wealth creation. This is not to say that such theorists do not also credit capitalism with other worthwhile traits, such as encouragement of progress, political liberty, innovation, etc.

Those who defend the system for its utilitarian virtues—its propensity to encourage the production of wealth—are distinct from others who champion the system—or the broader framework within which it exists—because they consider it morally just.

The first group of supporters argue that a free market or capitalist economic system is of great public benefit, even though this depends on private or even social vice, such as greed, ambition, or exploitation. As Bernard Mandeville, author of *The Fable of the Bees*, put it, this system produces "private vice, public benefit." Many moral theorists see nothing virtuous in efforts to improve one's own life. They believe, however, that enhancing the overall wealth of a human community is a worthwhile goal.

Those who stress the moral or normative merits of Capitalism (mostly libertarians) say the system rewards prudence, hard work, ingenuity, industry, entrepreneurship, and personal or individual responsibility in all spheres of human life, and this is all to the good. This alone makes the system morally preferable to alternatives. Yet, another reason given why libertarianism or capitalism is not only useful, but morally preferable, is that it makes possible the exercise of genuine moral choice and agency, something that would be obliterated in noncapitalist, collectivist systems or economic organization.

Capitalist theorists note that most critics of capitalism demean wealth. Indeed, they virtually attack the pursuit of human individual well-being itself, especially luxury, anytime there are needy people left anywhere on earth, as well as, more recently, if any portion of nature is overrun by human beings (as if they were not natural creatures). But, the champions of capitalism argue, this stems from utopian thinking, and has the consequence of begrudging anyone a measure of welfare, since some people will always be poor some of the time, and nature will continue to be transformed by people.

Yet the capitalist advocate need not be seen as reckless toward the environment. Indeed, arguably the strict and consistent institution of the principle of private property rights—through, for example, privatization and prohibition of dumping waste into other private, as well as public, realms—may solve the environmental problems we face better than any central planning champions of the environment tend to propose. Libertarians and capitalists think that the environment suffers more when the "tragedy of the commons" is permitted, whereby commonly owned values are overused, since everyone is deemed to have a right to such use, while no one in particular is left with the responsibility to care for it.

Capitalism rests in large part on the belief that human beings are essentially individuals, and a society's laws must value individuals above all else. Most historians of ideas admit that whether the importance of human individuality should have been recognized in earlier times, it certainly was not much heeded until the modern age. Even in our time, it is more often that groups—ethnic, religious, racial, sexual, national, cultural, etc.—are taken to have greater significance than individuals. The latter are constantly asked to make sacrifices for the former. In capitalism, however, the individual—e.g., as the sovereign citizen or the consumer—is king. Undoubtedly, a capitalist system does not give prime place to economic equality among people, something that group thinking seems to favor, since in groups, all are deemed entitled to a fair share.

Welfare Statism

The welfare state—or, from the economic viewpoint, the mixed economy—may be understood as a combination of the principles of capitalism and socialism. Sometimes the emphasis in this system is placed not so much on economic matters as on certain moral considerations. Basically, the welfare state consists of a legal system that aims at securing for everyone the negative right to liberty and the positive right to well-being.

The welfare state, which is to say most Western countries, balances the two values that together seem to be the bedrock of a civilized society to its advocates. No one should have his or her sovereignty seriously compromised, nor should anyone be permitted to fall below a certain standard of living. This is difficult to maintain, because at different times, one or another of these objectives will probably take priority, and in mostly democratic systems, political leaders will vacillate between giving more support to one or the other. The right to strike, for example, which is the negative liberty to quit one's job in an effort to gain respect for one's terms of employment, may conflict with the positive right to be provided with various services—e.g., health care, mail delivery, or education.

It is indeed a prominent feature of the welfare state that both negative and positive rights receive their legal protection. Negative rights involve respect for a person's life, liberty, and property—that is, everyone is by law supposed to abstain from interfering with these. Positive rights, in turn, involve respect for a person's basic needs—that is, everyone who is unable to secure the requirements of survival, and even flourishing, is supposed to have those provided by way of the appropriate public policy (e.g., taxation, mandated services, public education, national health care).

The moral underpinnings of the welfare state can be utilitarianism, altruism, or certain intuitively held moral precepts. Utilitarianism required that the general welfare be pursued by all, and whatever public policies needed to facilitate this would be justified. Although many utilitarians believe that the general welfare is best achieved when government operates in a largely laissez-faire fashion, there is no objection to government intervention in social affairs if without those, many in the society may fail to achieve a decent and prosperous form of life. Altruists, in turn, often hold that to make certain that people fulfill their primary obligation to help others, it is necessary to introduce public measures that will secure such help, given that many might wish to breach their duty to do the right thing. Finally, there is the claim that by our common intuition, it is evident that both a measure of personal liberty and social welfare must be guaranteed to all, lest the quality of life in society fall below what it should be.

While people object to the welfare state from several other perspectives, it is thought by its supporters to be the most stable modern political orders. Although it is characterized by much dispute and controversy, in the long run, its supporters maintain, the system seems to be satisfactory and just overall.

Communitarianism

Communitarianism could be viewed as a sort of halfway house between the collectivist system of socialism and the individualist one of capitalism. The idea is less capable of being sharply defined than these others. Roughly, it comes to the view that human beings are necessarily or essentially parts of distinct human groups, communities, with their diverse values, histories, priorities, practices, laws, cultures, etc. The organizing principles of these different groups will themselves vary. There is no overriding true social and political order, or even any universal ethics. Rather, it is the particular character of the communities that establish the proper way to live for its parts or members, what laws should be enacted, and what aesthetic and religious values need to be embraced.

Some communities can be Spartan, others stoic, still others bohemian, and so forth. Each can have its peculiar way of life without implying any objective condemnation of some alternative form. Yet participation in the community's form of life is not a matter of individual consent. Such an idea derives from a mistake: there is a transcendent or general human nature that requires every community to adhere to certain minimal standards of justice. No such transcendent human nature exists, as far as many communitarians see things, so those that, say, grant individuals certain rights are not superior to those that do not—they are simply different.[5]

Actually, there is not much more that can be said about communitarianism, because there are simply too many types of communities, each with its own framework and priorities. The main point is that the rules, laws, ideals, and so forth are all the result of the often slowly evolving consensus or collective practices of the community's membership. Just as socialism sees humanity as the whole to which individuals belong, communitarianism sees different ethnic, national, racial, gender, cultural, professional, or similar distinguishable groups as the whole to which the individual member belongs. One may imagine, for example, that languages have developed, in part, to meet the requirements, imagination, and circumstances of different linguistic communities, with no language superior or completely translatable to any other.

Communitarians often unite in their criticism of bourgeois society or liberal capitalism because of their emphasis on individuality, privacy, personal freedom, consent, competition, etc. Communitarians believe that the view of human nature underlying such liberal capitalist views is seriously flawed. They are also convinced that the central idea of liberal capitalism is what has come to be known as *homo economicus*, or "economic man." That idea figures heavily in economic analysis and views individuals as autonomous entities who enter the world fully formed, ready to make choices in the

---

5 For this line of communitarianism, see Richard Rorty, *Objectivity, Relativism, and Truth* (Cambridge, England: Cambridge University Press, 1991), especially "Solidarity or Objectivity" and "The Priority of Democracy to Philosophy." A somewhat different, though also less clear-cut, version of communitarianism is advanced by Amitai Etzioni, *The Spirit of Community* (New York: Crown Publishing Co., 1994).

market, and self-sufficient. While there are other conceptions of the human individual that might support liberal capitalism, it is this that has occupied the attention of communitarians. It is in contrast to this view that they have advanced their position.

Islamic Political Theory

Muslims are divided into two communities, the Sunni majority and Shiite minority, and they adhere to different ideas regarding political rule. They are known as the Sunni caliphate and the Shi'a Imamate.

When Muhammad died, most Muslims thought that Muhammad did not name a successor. They therefore relied upon the decision of a group of his cohorts. The caliphate, chosen by way of consultation (called *shura*) and agreement (called *ijma*), an oath of loyalty (called *baya*) that's sworn by those who elect him, and the compact (called *ahd*) with the people to govern by Islamic law (Sharia) developed into what is widely regarded as the legitimate government for Sunni Islam.

But the Shiites rejected the Sunni caliphs and saw them as subverting Islamic law. They adhered to the idea that Muhammad had selected Ali, who was reported to be his cousin and son-in-law, to be the ruler (*Imam*) of Muslims. They held that the oldest (male) descendant (*Ahl al-Bait*) must be the divinely anointed religious and political chief. Abbasid rule (750–1250) formed Islamic political theory as theocratic, with theologians as the legal authorities who had royal privilege, and professed to uphold the divine goal for the Muslim community under Abbasid edicts. In the last analysis, as matters now stand, there is no unified Muslim political theory that enjoys widespread acceptance.

In geopolitical affairs, a very influential version of Muslim politics comes from the clerics and adherents of the Wahhabi branch of radical Islam, based mainly in Saudi Arabia. Wahhabism is considered the most virulently anti-Western branch of Islam, in light of the belief that any accommodation of Western values is an intolerable compromise with the words of the Prophet. The main point of contention is that the West legally tolerates freedom of religion and even non-belief, which undermines the virtuous life demanded of the Islamic faithful, leading to their corruption.

Jewish Political Theory

Jews, as such, do not adhere to a firm political creed, unlike many Muslims, but tend to embrace varieties of democratic, even liberal, institutions, while also encouraging some Socialist economic practices and certain mild forms of theocracies, depending on the version of Judaism they embrace.

Jewish political ideas derive mainly from the belief that Jews are a separate, unique—chosen—people, not merely adherents to a different religion or a system of moral principles that emerge from such a religion. (Of course, this idea is shared by nearly all traditional and organized religious groups.) Jewish political ideas pertain to how the Jews as a unified people have held on to a political community throughout the centuries, without becoming amalgamated into communities where they lived as exiles, and how they shaped these by giving clear expressions of their own culture and forms of political conduct.

Jews often choose to demonstrate a Jewishness via political means. For many of them, this consists of loyalty to modern Israel, as well as various "Jewish" missions, including various communal groups (for example, the *kibbutz*) constituted almost exclusively by Jews. As is common in politics everywhere, Jews will often stress the need for power as they advance the causes of their various groupings, although this also includes extensive education and proselytizing.

Summary of Political Philosophers

Individual Political Thinkers:

The Greek soldier and philosopher **Alcibiades** (450–404 B.C.) appears to contend that the law that imposes unwanted behavior or institutions on people (those who do not consent) is either a bad law, or no law at all. This paves the earliest way toward either anarchism or minarchism. Just government must be minimal.

Socrates (470–399 B.C.E.) and *Plato* (c. 427–347 B.C.E.), relating Socrates' views, seeks to learn what is the best human life; uses society to investigate the topic (as a large model of the soul that's easily investigated). The result is that the person with a just soul—a soul that is in proper harmony, which has "got it together"—has its three components properly ordered. The highest component is reason (in society, the governor or king), the middle one is the emotions (the administrators and craftsmen in society), and the lowest are the instinct or drives (in society, the merchants or tradesmen). In a just person, reason must rule, the emotions must provide support, and the drives or instincts must keep the organism healthful.

Socrates would rather seek truth than take part in Politics, but his pupils coerce him to attend to politics, and he finally yields to the pressure; this suggests that Plato believed the philosopher must take part in politics so as to help figure out what is just, what is right; otherwise, the mob rules according to preferences rather than standards of justice.

It also seems Socrates has a very strict idea of what it is to know something, so he professes to know nothing; this suggests that Plato held that ultimate knowledge of things is impossible—or at least extremely hard. But this is not to be told to everyone, since people would become frightened if told that the wisest among them cannot know anything.

Aristotle (384–322 B.C.E.) approached understanding the world differently from Plato's Socrates, although he, too, prized reason as the primary means for this purpose. Unlike the idealist Plato, Aristotle was a naturalist—in both senses: that he studied nature, and he derived his view of human excellence based on what he knew about human nature (on what it is to be a human being). People are rational animals, and they are at their best when they activate their rational faculty to the utmost. They will, if they do this, practice the virtues—honesty, prudence, generosity, temperance, moderation, courage, and so forth. All these virtues are ways of acting that avoid extremes. Thus Aristotle's "doctrine of the mean."

When it comes to politics, the city for which one is seeking to find the best constitution is relatively small—about 1,000 people, most of them slaves (who are often families of POWs). Instead of developing an ideal polity, Aristotle studied existing cities in ancient Greece, and compared their constitutions in order to find out which one is best for human flourishing.

Aristotle is an elitist who thinks the best people ought to rule, but there is too much risk in this—they are tempted by power. So a constitution that leaves everyone able to take part in politics, a kind of constitutional republic, is the best regime. Government must encourage human virtue, be somewhat paternalistic. Aristotle explicitly rejects the libertarian idea that government should stay out of social life entirely and merely protect individual rights.

Aristotle sees problems with retail trade or commerce, because he believes that in exchange of goods, the values are all equal. (This, however, makes it mysterious why people would trade at all.)

St. Augustine (354–430 B.C.) was a dualist who believed that morality should guide us to save our everlasting, eternal souls, while politics must be pragmatic and make mundane life possible. The two should not mix. For those like Augustine, there is always the problem of just how the spiritual and the material realm interact at all. After all, the two are composed of drastically different types of substances. (We still struggle with this issue when we puzzle over how mind relates to body.) In a way, Augustine's politics exhibits this puzzle—citizens must seek to live right by standards that guide them to heaven, while they must also accommodate their mundane, earthly community needs.

Thomas Aquinas (1224–1274) was a 12th-century Roman Catholic theologian and saint who also studied Aristotle very closely. His main contribution was to argue that faith and reason are mutually reinforcing. What people believe by faith can, if right, be shown to be true by rational means—e.g., God's existence. Aquinas brought Aristotle's concern with nature—and science—into vogue so that the Catholic Church started to open the door to science. To this day, Roman Catholics claim to be able to reconcile science and religion. Aquinas also paved the way to opening markets and removing government regimentation of the economy, because he held that the just prices of commodities are best discovered by way of free market exchanges (via bargaining). Usury—earning money from lending it—though still a sin, became a less severe sin than before.

Niccolo Machiavelli (1469-1527), author of *The Prince* (a letter addressed to the ruler) was disenchanted with idealistic political thinking. He held that concerns about justice and virtue, especially in the Christian tradition, tended to weaken the government and society, which needed power most of all, to secure the freedom and independence of the country. The subsequent centuries have seen an ongoing struggle between the concerns of practical, effective governance versus the upholding of diverse standards of justice and decency. Today, for example, some argue that to fight terrorism or cope with the threat of environmental disaster, the government must follow precautionary measures and not be tied down by worries about individual rights, civil liberties, and similar concerns that tend to tie its hands. Others hold that a proper understanding of public morality favors Machiavelli's belief that prudence, most of all, must guide political leaders, and not, for example, the Christian virtue of charity.

Thomas Hobbes (1588-1679) is a major figure of modern philosophy. Hobbes rejected Aristotle—or at least the Aristotle of the Middle Ages—and introduced the scientific method into the study of human affairs (especially politics). Hobbes admired Galileo, and learned from him the method of reduction, looking for the smallest component of everything, identifying its principles of motion, and then inferring how other, larger entities would behave. Starting with the assumption that people, not unlike atoms, are motivated to progress, to move forward, and would in the state of nature eventually clash; so they need to find some way to get along—otherwise, they will destroy one another. From this, because of their intelligence, they would establish a social compact and natural laws (actually laws of convention). So that everyone obeys these laws, a king would be selected to enforce the laws, and the king would have to be obeyed, except when his policies posed deadly danger. (Check out the American Declaration of Independence for the influence of these ideas.)

Baruch Spinoza (1632-1677) produced one of the most impressive systematic philosophies in the history of the discipline, much of it in his books on ethics and political thought. His work was far reaching and very controversial—he identified God as nature, and was accused of atheism as a result.

Spinoza's political thought was distinctive in that it began a trend toward liberalism, in the classical sense of the term of freeing citizens from governmental intrusiveness. Although he shared Hobbes's idea that government has supreme authority, Spinoza counseled that there should be more trust in the judgment of the citizenry, especially when it comes to expressing opinions and engaging in commerce. One might say he was a very early precursor to public choice theory, the contemporary idea that government officials tend to favor their own interests as they make decisions purportedly in the public interest. Spinoza considered it wiser, more prudent to have the citizenry take more responsibility for the management of its affairs.

John Locke (1632–1704) was a British philosopher, Oxford academic, and medical researcher whose association with the first Earl of Shaftesbury led him to become a government official charged with collecting information about trade and colonies, an economic writer, opposition political activist, and finally, a revolutionary whose cause ultimately triumphed in the Glorious Revolution of 1688.

Locke's main contribution to political philosophy is his theory of natural individual rights. It had a major impact on the American founders, especially Thomas Jefferson. (Some dispute this, and claim Hobbes's influence was greater.)

Natural rights theory comes from natural law theories—both require one to study human nature so as to derive principles of human conduct. The natural rights approach focuses on principles of community life, while natural law focuses first and foremost on personal conduct. (There is also the phrase "natural *right*," but this means "correct by reference to human nature." It is used by the 20th-century political scientist, Leo Strauss.)

Locke identified adult human individuals as by nature—that is, as a matter of their basic humanity—"free and independent." This, he appears to have contended, would need to be accommodated in a just human community by respecting and protecting everyone's natural rights to "person and estate": that is, life, liberty and property. Governments are instituted among us so as to protect these rights—not for other purposes—from domestic criminals and foreign aggressors. Government's conduct must itself respect these rights. Many echoes of these ideas are evident throughout American law, and even the politics of the West. Today, libertarians are the ones who are mainly loyal to Locke's ideas. Unlike some contemporary political and legal theorists, Locke considered our rights to be pre-political and pre-legal, to which politics and law need to be faithfully adjusted.

David Hume (1711–1776) was born to a moderately wealthy family from Berwickshire, Scotland, near Edinburgh. He is best dubbed a major conservative and skeptical thinker who taught us to distrust rationalistic thinking (modeling the way we understand everything on logic, Mathematics, and geometry). Because Hume distrusted reasoning about things, he thought it best to study tradition and history to learn how we ought to act and organize our communities. If we did this conscientiously, we would benefit the most. Such virtues as justice, prudence, and respect for private property will serve us well by leading to peace and prosperity. Hume was the first major philosopher to embrace commerce as a decent part of society. Hume is also famous for identifying the "is-ought gap," the view that no deduction of moral judgments is possible based on factual judgments. In science, the laws of nature are more like our expectations than firm causal laws.

Adam Smith (1723–1790) was a Scottish moral philosopher whose work became one of the foundations of modern economic science. His studies of economic matters led him to favor nearly completely free markets and laissez-faire policies—"leave us alone"— where political economy is concerned (although there is some debate about this). Smith identified the *principle of natural liberty* as best suited to promote prosperity for an entire nation—all this is in his most famous book, *The Wealth of Nations* (published in 1776). (He actually liked his other major work, *The Theory of Moral Sentiments* [1759] better.) Smith supported markets not from the basis of natural rights (as Locke did), but because they would be better for economic progress, all things considered. He also promoted the notion, new in his era, that trade is a win-win, not a zero-sum, relationship between people—both are likely to get what they want from it, and there need be no losers. That also led him to promote peace among nations: do not try to enrich your country by conquest, but by trade. The idea that trade involves rip-offs or exploitation is widely believed, mainly under the influence of Karl Marx and his followers, but Smith would have disputed this.

Jean-Jacques Rousseau (1712–1778) is well known for his concern with how society has corrupted human beings over the centuries, how "Man is born free, but everywhere he is in chains." His main contribution to political philosophy is that the standard by which societies ought to be organized is what would be commanded by "the general will." This is not the majority or the unanimous decision of the members or citizens, but what a citizenry would want were it to have a clear and virtuous idea of itself. It is a difficult notion to fill in, although most of us are somewhat familiar with it from our own experience with how our conscience looks over and critically assesses our actions, from how we sense that there is a best within us that could become dominant in our lives.

Rousseau thought that in our original state or state of nature, we are innocent—even basically good—but as we develop and interact with society, we begin to lose this innocence and goodness. There is an intimation of the noble savage idea here. Problem is, it doesn't quite explain why, if we are born so fine, we go so bad in time. Society, after all, is made up of a lot of us, so how did it get corrupted?

In the last analysis, Rousseau's improved society is a highly regimented one, where freedom means ordered freedom, freedom that is disciplined by virtue, where a one-size-fits-all idea of how human beings ought to be governs.

Edmund Burke (1729–1797) is best remembered for his strong conservative ideas, although some of his conclusions fit well within the English Whig political faction that had a classical liberal thrust and was critical of Britain's abuse of its American colonies. Burke laid out a conservative approach to politics, a little like David Hume, emphasizing the need to consult tradition rather than rely on an individual's reasoning (as radical thinkers urge us to do). As he put it, "... Men have no right to risk the very existence of their nation and their civilization upon experiments in morals and politics; for each man's private capital of intelligence is petty; it is only when a man draws upon the bank and capital of the ages, the wisdom of our ancestors, that he can act wisely." [Quoted in Kenneth M. Dolbeare, *Directions of American Political Thought* (New York: John Wiley & Sons, Inc., 1969), p. 11).] He also made the point that "We are afraid to put men to live and trade each on his own private stock of reason, because we suspect that this stock in each man is small, and that the individuals would do better to avail themselves of the general bank of nations and of ages." [*Reflections on the Revolution in France* (Indianapolis: Hackett Publishing Co., 1987), p. 76.]

Immanuel Kant (1724–1804) brought about what is called a "Copernican Revolution" in philosophy, after his reading of David Hume led him to be "woken from his dogmatic slumbers." That is, he argued against skepticism by concluding that the human mind was guided by innate, necessary categories (causality, quantity, quality, etc.) that led us to organize our sensory experiences in certain ways. He proposed that reality is made of the phenomenal and the noumenal realms, the first studied by sciences, the second by philosophy and theology. The first relies on evidence from the senses; the second deals with assumptions we must make for reality to make sense for us.

For Kant, a central issue in moral philosophy is personal autonomy—only those who govern themselves can be morally responsible. So a society must forge laws that protect and preserve personal autonomy. Kant coined the phrase "ought implies can," which means that for morality to make any sense, human beings must be free to choose.

In light of these—often very complex—reflections, Kant became very influential in philosophy. He was one of the supporters of classical liberal politics.

The Federalist Papers were a series of articles written under the pen name of Publius by Alexander Hamilton, James Madison, and John Jay just prior to the American Revolution. Madison, dubbed the Father of the Constitution, later went on to become an early president of the United States. Jay, the first chief justice of the U.S. Supreme Court, and Hamilton later served in the Cabinet, becoming dominant in devising economic policy for the new United States of America. (Read more about all this at http://www.law.ou.edu/hist/federalist/)

The main objective of The Federalist Papers was to lay the groundwork for the kind of constitution the new country should have. There was fairly wide agreement that the country should not be a monarchy, or anything close to it—as evidenced by what is contained in the Declaration of Independence—but how that was to be accomplished took a lot of deliberation, argument, speculation, and so forth.

The authors, all well educated in the history of political thought, forged the idea of the separation and balance of powers—the legislative, executive, and judicial branch of the federal (and indeed any) branches—that would keep government from becoming tyrannical. This balance of powers would prevent any one branch from dominating public policy.

Overall, there is no scholarly consensus on how well they succeeded, since many today think that the federal government is too powerful and its scope far beyond what the founders envisioned, although others hold that the changes in the world over the last two centuries made this necessary. The founders and framers pretty much would have expected this, had they known of all the developments over the years.

Georg Wilhelm Friedrich Hegel (1770–1831) is most famous for his dialectical idealist metaphysics; he argued that dialectics is a feature of the world's development (not, like Plato taught, a feature of how we should learn about the world). A process of dialectical development unfolds in history, bringing the idea of reality and actuality closer and closer, headed for a perfect union, thus exhibiting progress. In politics, Hegel thought Prussia had already reached this perfect state.

For Hegel, Christianity is a kind of "metaphysics lite," meaning it tells in simple terms how the world developed. The dialectical process involves a state of affairs which then gives rise to its opposite state of affairs, and from the clash of the two, a third state of affairs emerges, only to be repeated until the perfect state is reached. (Thesis versus antithesis, resulting in a synthesis, and on and on.) All events develop in this fashion; nothing is accidental; all philosophy mirrors this, and leads to Hegel's final perfect philosophical system.

Politically, too, all previous ways of community living aim for the final politics that was to be Prussia's empire.

Karl Marx (1818–1883) adopted some of Hegel's notions, especially the dialectic, as a heuristic tool (something that has a useful purpose in understanding things, but not, as Hegel thought, a metaphysical principle). Marx, however, was not an idealist, but a materialist—so his position got the name "dialectical materialism."

The dialectic is a process of a thesis, in the history of the world—but mostly in human history—that creates its opposite state, an antithesis. Then, after the clash, this reaches a culmination in a synthesis; this continues until reality or humanity is emancipated (in communism). This is a deterministic system, although minor instances of human freedom are possible, albeit inconsequential. Marx saw humanity as we see a person—with its infancy (the tribal era), childhood (feudal era), adolescence (the capitalist stage), young adulthood (socialism), and maturity (communism). Each turns into the next by means of revolution (but not always a violent one).

Marx believed that those who see capitalism as the right socioeconomic system mistake a stage for the end. Like thinking of adolescence as if it were maturity. Capitalism still involves alienation (being a stranger to ourselves because of all kinds of inner conflicts in the system). The capitalists must necessarily exploit the workers, until the workers revolt and overthrow the system. This comes about when workers become intolerant with the anarchy of the market system, and finally abolish private property.

John Stuart Mill (1806–1873), the major utilitarian in Western philosophy, supported a pretty strict (but not radical) market system (like Adam Smith, but less radical than John Locke). Mill believed that such a system is superior in its productivity to all others, including socialism. The ultimate goal to strive for is "the greatest happiness of the greatest number," but happiness must include autonomy or individual liberty, so here he is closer to Locke than other utilitarians. Individual rights to life, liberty, etc., facilitate reaching the goal of that greatest happiness, because they unleash productivity. There are a few cases in which state planning is justified, as with public utilities. (Delivering these in a market would be wasteful.) Mill's "simple principle" is very famous. It states "[T]he sole end for which mankind are warranted, individually or collectively in interfering with the liberty of action of any of their number, is self-protection." (*On Liberty*, p. 16.) Late in his life Mill became more sympathetic to government intervention not in the production but the distribution end of the economy.

Mary Shelley Wollstonecraft (1797–1851) was an early advocate of the emancipation of women. She wrote eloquently in support of a moral life, which, however, she believed might have to be required of everyone. She was also an ethical vegetarian, or what is today called a "vegan." Shelley Wollstonecraft's beliefs tended toward socialism, because it had been socialists who were most concerned with women's rights.

Thomas Hill Green (1836–1882) was a right-wing Hegelian political thinker who believed in a highly ordered state. Thus, regarding laws, individuals ideally should see them as external expressions of their own true will. So, if the law is good, by following it, one just follows one's own true will. Law reflects, primarily, the abstract idea of a human being as the "self-conscious and self-realising subject" whose failings (desires which do not push him to realize his proper ends in life) must be restrained to enable the will's "attainment of its own perfection." By following the law, individuals acknowledge their own ability to become what they are not at present. Law also must also assist us to reinforce our true values, which express the actions of the eternal consciousness as it is found in our world. Thus, we are gradually aligned with "the law of [our] being."

Herbert Spencer (1820–1903) was a believer in the historical progress of humanity toward a fully individualist, libertarian society. A great believer in science, Spencer's name is often linked with the idea of social Darwinism, the notion that societies should permit the principle of the survival of the fittest to operate, so those who fail should be left to wither away, while those who succeed should be supported. Spencer wasn't actually a heartless thinker, but he did think that the poor were often complicit in their poverty and did not deserve all the pity they received.

Mikhail Bakunin's (1814–1876) political beliefs completely opposed governing systems, from those of God all the way down. He denied all forms of external authority, whether coming from the will of a leader or a monarch, or from voters. Bakunin said, „The liberty of man consists solely in this, that he obeys the laws of nature, because he has himself recognized them as such, and not because they have been imposed upon him externally by any foreign will whatsoever, human or divine, collective or individual." Since natural laws are recognized by everyone for oneself, Bakunin reasoned, a person could not help but obey them. They would be laws of one's very own nature. So he favored anarchism, with no need for political organization, administration, or legislation.

John Dewey (1859–1952) was a major figure in the pragmatist movement. Pragmatism is one of the very few American homegrown philosophical schools, begun by Charles Sanders Peirce in the late 1800s. Several other important members are C. I. Lewis, William James, and more recently, Willard Quine, and today, the radical pragmatist Richard Rorty.

A major theme of pragmatism is that philosophies that have tried to find fundamental principles from which to secure support for their ideas have failed—most notably René Descartes, the French founder of modern philosophy. So pragmatism is very skeptical about foundations. The basis of claiming one knows something, therefore, cannot be that it is well founded, but that when one uses it to guide action, things work out better than otherwise. "Pragmatic," then, tends to mean "practical" or "workable."

For political purposes, this means that pragmatists avoid strict adherence to basic principles, such as those stated in the Declaration of Independence. Dewey, in particular, wanted to have a society that is a compromise between capitalism and socialism, the kind of welfare state we actually live in now, more or less.

Benito Mussolini (1883–1945), the fascist dictator of Italy in the 1930s, was not a philosopher, but he did write on politics and advocated fascism, which is a system that mostly relies on the inspired leadership of a charismatic leader. (Other fascists are Hitler, Pinochet, Peron, and even Saddam Hussein.) Fascist leaders do not adhere to some clear political theory, such as socialism or capitalism, and tend to vary on what they think best for their society. Mussolini preferred what is called guild socialism, a socialist system that consisted of the several groups of trade unions, and managed the Italian economy based on their goals. (Hitler preferred national socialism, Peron popular democracy, while Pinochet liked a largely capitalist military dictatorship.)

Vladimir Lenin (1870–1924), the first leader of the Soviet Union, revised Marx's idea that the working class would usher in the revolution that would move society from a capitalist to a socialist political-economic system. Lenin saw that the workers did not take up their leadership roles, and so he believed they needed to be guided by Bolshevik intellectuals. It is with this guidance that socialism, and eventually, communism, would be achieved. These intellectuals would be "history's little helpers."

Friedrich A. Hayek (1899–1992), an Austrian-born Nobel Prize winner (1974) in economics, was a student of Ludwig von Mises. Both championed the free market system and began with a criticism of socialism, arguing that that system is unable to solve the "economic calculation problem." This is to figure out what and how much needs to be produced, and by whom and where it will be consumed. Socialism proposes to figure this out from the planner's offices. But Hayek and von Mises argued that the information needed to establish this is, in principle, unavailable to planners, since they aren't where the action is: namely, in the market place. People in free markets spend their resources on what they want, which gives those who produce things the needed knowledge to decide what and how much of it, at what price, to produce. They will know whether the needed raw materials, labor, time, and skills are available, so they will also be able to put an economic value on these things. Supply and demand can, thus, be coordinated without anyone doing any top-down planning.

Hayek argued also that instead of government, central planning to achieve order, and a rational system, such order will emerge spontaneously, based on the free choices/decisions of market agents. This will not always be "fair" (say, as James P. Sterba wishes), but it will be immensely more productive than the so-called fair system of socialism can be. (And because of the police power needed to carry through a planned fair system, it will never be a fair system, anyway.)

Additionally, Hayek argued for gradual cultural evolution to give us technological, artistic, scientific, and related progress, coming from people interacting freely. His major books are *Road to Serfdom*; *The Constitution of Liberty*; *Law, Legislation, and Liberty*; and *The Fatal Conceit*.

Milton Friedman (1912–2006) was the leader of the Chicago School of (neoclassical) Economics. He was one of the most important contemporary representatives of a certain branch of classical liberalism. Author of *Capitalism and Freedom* (1962) and *Free to Choose* (1980), as well as many technical works in economics, Friedman supported free enterprise and strictly limited government as the most efficient political economic system. He held that values were subjective, so criticizing what people do in the market place as they wheel and deal, aside from violating rights, is impossible. (Values or utilities are incapable of interpersonal comparisons.)

Friedman and Hayek founded the Mont Pelerin Society, an international organization of classical liberals. (Classical liberals emphasize negative freedom, whereby people must not interfere with each other unless there is mutual agreement; modern liberalism involves using the government and public policy—wealth redistribution—to set people free to pursue their various goals.)

Ayn Rand (1905–1982) was born in Russia and immigrated to the United States in the 1920s. She wanted to write novels, but decided that to do this properly she needed to fully, philosophically, examine the nature of human life. The result was her philosophy, Objectivism. Rand's novels, *We The Living*, *Anthem*, *The Fountainhead*, and *Atlas Shrugged*, are not only stories, but carry a clear-cut philosophical message, which favors ideas, such as reality exists independently of our wishes, thoughts, hopes, etc.;

the human mind can (even if it does not often) know reality as it is, without distorting it; human beings ought to live by the guidance of their central and unique attribute—reason—which will lead them to the best, happiest life possible; the kind of community that accommodates this is the free society as John Locke and some other classical liberals understood it, with a capitalist economic system; and the arts ought to present and depict the highest conception of reality and human life. Rand also wrote *Capitalism: The Unknown Ideal*, which contains most of her political philosophical work.

Leo Strauss (1899–1973), was a German-born political philosopher who also emigrated to the United States. He taught that modern philosophy lost something important when Hobbes and others began to question that human nature is real, and suggested we invent the nature of things, not discover them. He thought that, in order to remedy this, philosophers need to rediscover the ancients—Socrates, Plato, Aristotle, and so forth. But Strauss also seemed to believe that real, serious philosophy is very risky, and may need to be hidden or disguised from ordinary people, who would fall apart knowing the uncertainty of things as philosophers do. Strauss's view was that philosophy is, nonetheless, very important, because it is the only road to genuine, ultimate truth, if there is any such thing. In any case, the philosophical life is the most precious, and only in a liberal society can it be pursued, so liberal societies need to be promoted, maybe even in an aggressive foreign policy. This is why Strauss is often associated with neoconservatism and George W. Bush's foreign policy. Strauss wrote the influential books *Natural Right and History* and *What Is Political Philosophy* (sections of which are in our text), among many other works.

John Rawls (1921–2002) was the 20th century's most prominent political philosopher. Teaching at Harvard University, he wrote *A Theory of Justice* (Harvard University Press, 1971), in which he advanced the idea that, contrary to what the positivists had believed, ethics and politics are possible. Their basic premises rest on universal human intuitions. These intuitions support the welfare state.

Using the method of the hypothetical social contract, Rawls imagines a group of people deliberating "behind a veil of ignorance" and relying on these basic moral intuitions—the importance of personal liberty and of social-economic security. What comes out of this is that a just society would prize fairness above all (except when unfairness improves everyone's life).

Robert Nozick (1938–2002), also from Harvard, quickly replied to Rawls with his book *Anarchy, State, and Utopia* (Basic Books, 1974). He argued that if Rawls's idea that justice is fairness is accepted as the guide to public policy, a strong policy state would need to emerge, which clearly contradicts our intuitions. Each time people decide to give their resources to someone they prized highly—a basketball player or movie star or rock group—immediately thereafter the government would need to come in to readjust the way wealth is distributed, because those receiving the resources would be vastly richer than others. And this constant readjustment would be intolerable. So, Nozick argued, the only just society is one in which consensual relationships dominate. He held that a minarchist system would be just. Anarchism is too unstable, and would, Nozick believed, turn into minarchism.

Murray N. Rothbard (1926–1995) was an individualist anarchist, and Nozick started his own book by addressing Rothbard's arguments. Rothbard held that *all* governments are coercive by definition—they all must violate individual rights—so only anarchism can be just. He advocated competing defense or justice agencies that can exist side by side, so none would gain a monopoly status. His *Man, Economy, and State* and *Ethics of Liberty* contain elaborate arguments in defense of his position.

Susan Mendus objects to the underlying view of human nature that the three previous thinkers accept: namely, individualism. She holds that, in fact, we are almost totally intertwined with others, to form a network of human connections. Just as a beehive or ant colony looks like it has many individuals in it, in fact they all form a collective entity (the hive or the colony), so human individuals only *appear* independent, and, in fact, form a society. So the entire modern and classical liberal project is misguided; instead, a communitarian social order is proper.

Jurgen Habermas advocates total democracy—everyone must take part in the discourse about ethics and politics. But before that, certain conditions need to be established that will enable us all to be part of the democratic process. That means a kind of welfare state is necessary, even before democracy can commence.

Richard Rorty (1931–2007) was a radical pragmatist-communitarian who held that no objective perspective is possible by which to compare and evaluate different cultures and political societies/systems. We are all guided to think as we do by what our communities hold to be true. For each of us, the terms of our communities establish our values, even scientific truths. Comparisons are not possible, although everyone will quite honestly favor the terms of his or her own community—ethically, politically, aesthetically, and so forth.

Among some other contemporary political philosophers who could be discussed, the most important ones are Michael J. Sandel, Amartya Sen, John Hospers, Ronald Dworkin, *et al.*

Conclusion

None of the systems or positions sketched here are fully exemplified anywhere, although some—for example, Islamic theocracy—are approximated in some parts of the world (e.g., Iran). There are, however, no purely capitalist or Socialist or Communist societies, and the welfare states are also quite different, with various ways of balancing the values of personal autonomy and social security. Instead, most societies—countries—exhibit mixed systems. Often, where democratic decision making takes place, the main topic of debate is which of these values should be stressed more, as well as how much state support should be given to various special interests.

For most individuals, it is probably a hardship to become familiar with all these political viewpoints and their support, but in democracies, especially, some familiarity is unavoidable, just as a matter of conscientious citizenship. This is one reason why the study of the history of political philosophy is vital.

www.ingramcontent.com/pod-product-compliance
Lightning Source LLC
Chambersburg PA
CBHW080846020526
44114CB00045B/2681